Little Guides to
Great Lives

STEPHEN HAWKING

LAURENCE KING

Published in 2019 by Laurence King Publishing Ltd
361–373 City Road
London EC1V 1LR
United Kingdom
Tel: +44 20 7841 6900
e-mail: enquiries@laurenceking.com
www.laurenceking.com

Illustrations © 2019 Marianna Madriz
Text © 2019 Isabel Thomas

A catalog record for this book is available
from the British Library

ISBN: 978-1-78627-515-8

Commissioning editors: Chloë Pursey and Leah Willey
Senior editor: Felicity Maunder
Design concept: Charlotte Bolton
Design: Stuart Dando
Series title designed by Anke Weckmann

Printed in China

Laurence King Publishing is committed to ethical and
sustainable production. We are proud participants in
The Book Chain Project ®
bookchainproject.com

BOOK
CHAIN
PROJECT

Little Guides to Great Lives

STEPHEN
HAWKING

Written by
Isabel Thomas

Illustrations by
Marianna Madriz

Laurence King Publishing

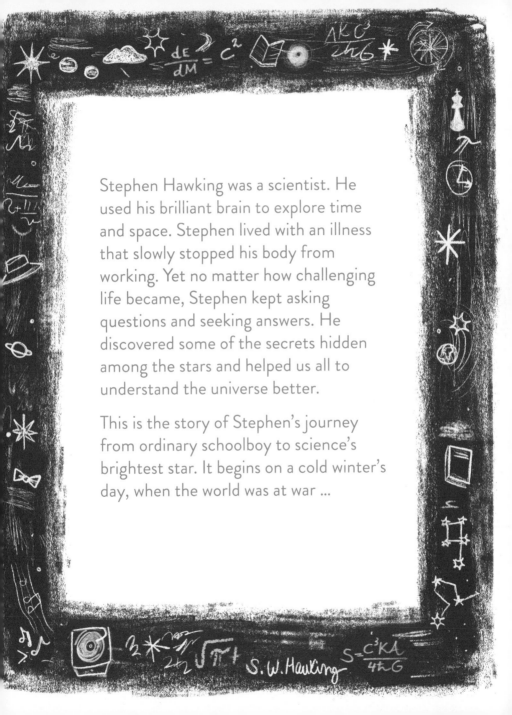

Stephen Hawking was a scientist. He used his brilliant brain to explore time and space. Stephen lived with an illness that slowly stopped his body from working. Yet no matter how challenging life became, Stephen kept asking questions and seeking answers. He discovered some of the secrets hidden among the stars and helped us all to understand the universe better.

This is the story of Stephen's journey from ordinary schoolboy to science's brightest star. It begins on a cold winter's day, when the world was at war ...

Stephen was born in January 1942, in the middle of World War Two. His family lived in London, which was often bombed by enemy planes in the first three and a half years of Stephen's life. He even remembered playing in the bombed-out ruins of a neighbor's house.

Frank Hawking
(a doctor who studied
tropical medicine)

Isobel Hawking
(a tax inspector turned
medical secretary)

Edward

Mary

A few years after the war ended, the Hawkings moved to a much smaller city called St Albans.

Stephen's parents were very interested in the world around them, and the whole family loved to read books— often they would all read together at the dinner table.

Stephen

Philippa

As a child, Stephen was always busy! He loved ...

... dancing,

... finding exciting ways
to climb into the house,

... board games

... and model trains,
planes, and boats.

Most of all, he loved
tinkering with complicated
things to find out how
they worked.

Stephen often found school too easy and too boring,
so he didn't work very hard.

The true sign of intelligence is not knowledge, but imagination.

Albert Einstein

While Stephen was at school, Albert Einstein was the world's most famous living scientist. He had won a <u>Nobel Prize</u> for explaining how space, time, and <u>gravity</u> work. His explanation is called the <u>general theory of relativity</u>. Most people didn't understand the general theory of relativity, but they did know the name "Einstein" meant "genius"!

As he got older, Stephen was sometimes embarrassed by his <u>eccentric</u> family, who drove an old taxicab instead of a normal car ...

... but mostly he enjoyed the opportunities they gave him to discover the world outside school. He spent time in Majorca and India, and visited the laboratory where his father was finding cures for nasty tropical diseases.

Stephen's father wanted him to study medicine, but Stephen didn't want to spend his life thinking about small things like human beings. He was interested in the biggest, most complicated thing of all ... the universe! When he was just 17, Stephen accepted a place at the University of Oxford to study <u>physics</u>.

At university, Stephen was taught by some of the world's best <u>physicists</u>, but he still found the work easy! He could whiz through complicated calculations without much effort, so he hardly tried at all.

Other parts of life were much harder. At first, Stephen felt lonely, and spent hours sitting in his room.

I'm shy and tongue-tied at times. I find it difficult to talk to people I don't know.

Eventually Stephen worked up the courage to join in with rowing. This helped him to make friends and have fun.

After three years of learning what other physicists had found out, Stephen was ready to join the hunt for answers himself.

He moved to the University of Cambridge to learn how to carry out <u>research</u>.

Stephen's favorite part of physics was cosmology—the study of how the universe began and developed. Cosmologists ask some of the BIGGEST questions of all ...

Has the universe always been like it is today ... or is it changing?

Did the universe have a beginning? Will it have an end?

Where did all the stars and galaxies come from?

Physicists can find answers in two different ways.

Experimental physicists discover the secrets of the universe by looking at objects in space. They look carefully at the light (and other types of rays) given out by stars and galaxies and they hunt for clues that will tell them what is going on.

Careful observations and experiments helped me to discover very <u>dense</u>, spinning stars called pulsars!

Jocelyn Bell Burnell, Experimental physicist

Theoretical physicists don't peer through telescopes or collect data. They try to describe and explain the universe using mathematics. Their calculations help them to come up with new ways of thinking and predict new phenomena.

I came up with the idea that objects are attracted toward each other by a force called gravity. The bigger an object, the stronger its gravity! I also came up with three simple laws that can predict how objects move.

Isaac Newton, Theoretical physicist

Stephen wanted to be a theoretical physicist and come up with big ideas about the universe. There was just one problem—he would have to get much better at math!

Stephen began teaching himself the tricky math needed to understand Einstein's general theory of relativity.

Einstein had realized that we can't *just* use Newton's simple laws to explain how things move. An object can seem to move in a completely different way depending on where you are standing. Even time is not a fixed thing! Our measurements of time depend on how we are moving relative to other things.

Einstein said that we should stop thinking of space and time as two separate things, and think of them as part of the same thing—space-time.

Every object in the universe—from the smallest atom to the biggest star—affects the shape of the space-time around it. The more massive an object is, the more it bends space-time. When a planet, a spacecraft, or a ray of light travels through this bent space-time, the path of the planet, spacecraft, or light bends too. This is the effect that we call gravity.

Stephen was beginning to understand the laws that predict how the universe works, when something completely unpredictable happened to him ...

For two years, Stephen had noticed himself getting clumsier. It became harder to climb trees and he had a nasty fall down a stone staircase. At home in St Albans, he fell over while ice skating and couldn't get up.

Stephen told his mother about his worries, and she encouraged him to see a doctor. After weeks of tests, Stephen was diagnosed with a rare and serious illness.

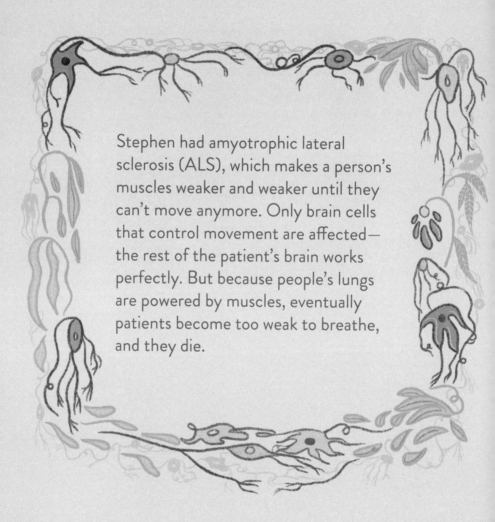

Stephen had amyotrophic lateral sclerosis (ALS), which makes a person's muscles weaker and weaker until they can't move anymore. Only brain cells that control movement are affected— the rest of the patient's brain works perfectly. But because people's lungs are powered by muscles, eventually patients become too weak to breathe, and they die.

Stephen wanted to know whether the universe had a beginning, and whether it will have an end.

In the 1960s, physicists had two very different theories about this. Some thought that the universe has no beginning or end and that it has always been like it is today.

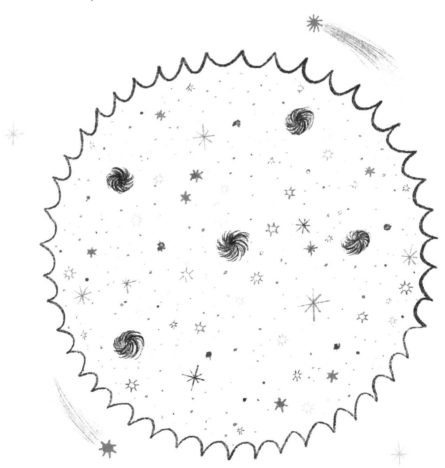

Others thought that the universe began around 14 billion years ago, with a "Big Bang," which produced all the energy, space, and <u>matter</u>. Since the Big Bang, the universe has been expanding, and cooling down.

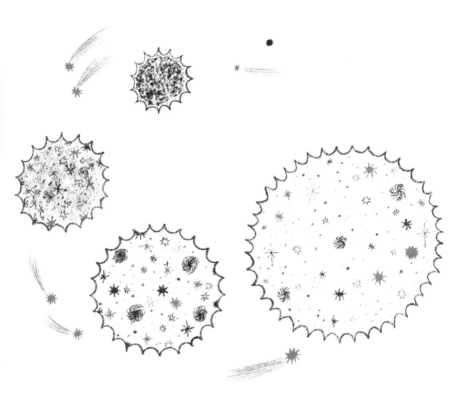

We may never know for sure which idea is right, because we can't travel back billions of years. But we can look for clues that tell us which theory is most likely to be right.

While Stephen was thinking about these big questions, his disease was developing much more slowly than his doctors had expected, but it was beginning to affect more of his body, making it hard for him to walk, write, or type. When he needed help, he asked the people around him. One of the most important was his wife, Jane.

Jane Wilde
(languages student)

Jane grew up in St Albans too, but met Stephen when he was studying at Cambridge. She liked the way Stephen could laugh about life's difficulties. Jane married Stephen in 1965. They soon had two children, Robert and Lucy.

Together with another brilliant scientist called Roger
Penrose, Stephen slowly began to unlock the secrets
of the structure of the universe. In Einstein's general
theory of relativity, Roger and Stephen found clues
to support the Big Bang theory.

Before the Big Bang, everything in
the universe must have been packed into an incredibly
tiny, hot speck known as a singularity.

You don't have to go back billions of years to find a singularity. They are also formed when massive stars run out of fuel and collapse. All the stuff that the star is made of gets squashed into a tiny space ...

... a bit like packing the whole of planet Earth into a space the size of a pea!

It's possible, because atoms are mostly empty space!

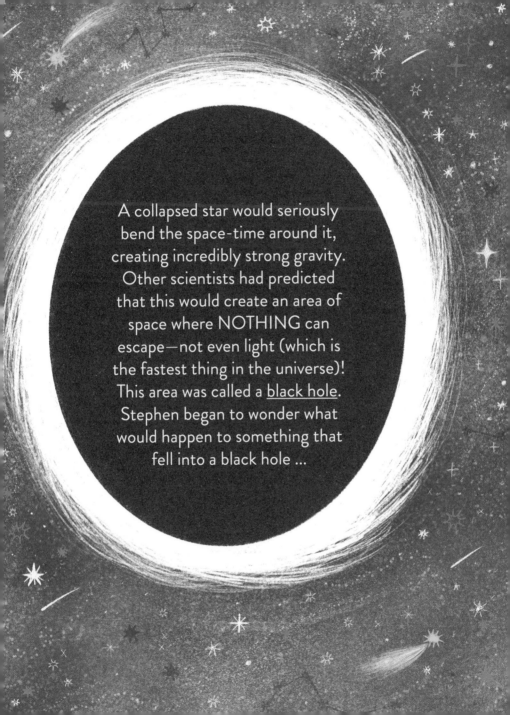

A collapsed star would seriously bend the space-time around it, creating incredibly strong gravity. Other scientists had predicted that this would create an area of space where NOTHING can escape—not even light (which is the fastest thing in the universe)! This area was called a <u>black hole</u>. Stephen began to wonder what would happen to something that fell into a black hole ...

Even for a supermassive brain like Stephen's, this was a difficult question. There are billions of supermassive stars in the universe, so there are probably billions of black holes too. The problem is, we can't see them! No light can escape, making black holes invisible to eyes, cameras, and telescopes.

That didn't matter to Stephen. He wasn't the kind of scientist who stares through telescopes. He could visit black holes in his mind and use math to work out what he might find there. Stephen decided to start by working out how tiny <u>particles</u> would behave near a black hole.

The math that Stephen knew best—Einstein's general theory of relativity—is only good at telling us about the BIGGEST objects in the universe. Stephen would have to use a completely different set of ideas. These ideas are called ...

QUANTUM THEORY

Quantum theory tells us about the tiniest particles in the universe, and how they behave.

Stephen worked so hard, he could hardly think of anything else. He built models of the universe in his mind, and spent hours exploring them.

After months of thinking, Stephen noticed something unexpected. His calculations were telling him that some particles CAN escape from black holes. But this was supposed to be impossible! Stephen checked his work for mistakes, but he couldn't find any.

When Stephen told other physicists about his discovery,
they were shocked too!

Quantum theory tells me that black holes aren't really black at all! I predict that particles DO escape over time. Eventually, a black hole will shrink so much, it will disappear!

But when other scientists looked carefully at Stephen's work, they agreed that his ideas seemed right. The leaking particles that Stephen had predicted were named "Hawking radiation."

Stephen had developed a brand new way of thinking about black holes, and had predicted how they might change over time. Excitingly, he had done this by bringing together ideas from two very different areas of physics, which had been seen as completely separate: general relativity and quantum theory.

Stephen was invited to join the Royal Society—a club for the world's greatest scientists. He was one of the youngest ever members! He was also invited to work at the California Institute of Technology (Caltech), in the USA.

At Caltech, Stephen worked on a new question ...

Hawking radiation was very weak, so it would be hard to spot among all the other rays and particles zooming across space—just as sunlight drowns out the faint light of other stars during the day. No matter how hard they looked, astronomers couldn't find any proof of Hawking radiation, or a real black hole.

Jane, Robert, and Lucy went to California too. When they were there, the family got a color TV for the first time. Stephen was also given an electric wheelchair. Now he could zoom around at the flick of a switch.

When the Hawking family moved back to England, Stephen was 33. His disease was still progressing much more slowly than doctors had first predicted, but his muscles were now too weak for him to climb stairs. Stephen also needed more help doing everyday things, but he did not want to live with nurses. He asked family, students, and colleagues to help him instead.

Stephen's brilliant brain was as strong as ever. In 1979, he was given one of the top science jobs in the world— Lucasian Professor of Mathematics at the University of Cambridge.

He won many awards throughout his life, including the Royal Society's top award—the Copley Medal—and the Breakthrough Prize in Fundamental Physics, with prize money of millions!

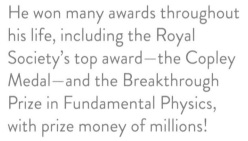

Stephen loved to travel. In 1985 he was visiting a famous <u>particle accelerator</u> in Switzerland, when he became very ill with <u>pneumonia</u>.

The doctors expected him to die, but Stephen refused to give up. So did Jane. She had Stephen flown back to Cambridge, where doctors made a permanent hole in his throat to help him breathe.

The operation saved Stephen's life ...

... but damaged his throat so much, he would never be able to speak again.

News spread quickly. A scientist in California sent him the latest technology—a computer program that let Stephen spell out words and sentences on a screen, using a switch in his hand.

Even better, it sent the finished sentences to a speech synthesizer—a machine that could speak his words. Stephen knew just what he wanted to say:

Before he got pneumonia, Stephen had been writing a book about the universe for people who weren't scientists. He wanted to explain how physicists were trying to answer the biggest, most difficult questions in the world.

Stephen finished his first draft in 1984. He was really pleased with it, but his <u>editor</u> wasn't!

The book needs lots of work. In fact, it needs completely rewriting to make it easier to understand!

Even now he had lost his voice forever, Stephen didn't give up. He just had to work more slowly, with support from the people around him. Letter by letter, word by word, Stephen gradually finished the book.

A Brief History of Time became a <u>bestseller</u> around the world.

Stephen was right— EVERYONE was interested in the universe.

People were also interested in Stephen's story. They wanted to know how he had overcome the challenges of his disability.

Stephen became a star! He enjoyed the fun of being rich and famous ...

... but for Jane it was hard. By now, Jane and Stephen had three children. For a long time, Jane had been feeling <u>depressed</u>, and worried about the future.

Now the world's media were orbiting their home and peering into their lives. Jane and Stephen separated in 1990 and were divorced in 1995. They both fell in love with new people and married again.

By now, Stephen's disease meant that he needed help and care 24 hours a day, but he kept tackling the hardest questions about space and time. Like ...

Did time exist before the Big Bang?

What shape is the universe?

Is it possible to travel in time?

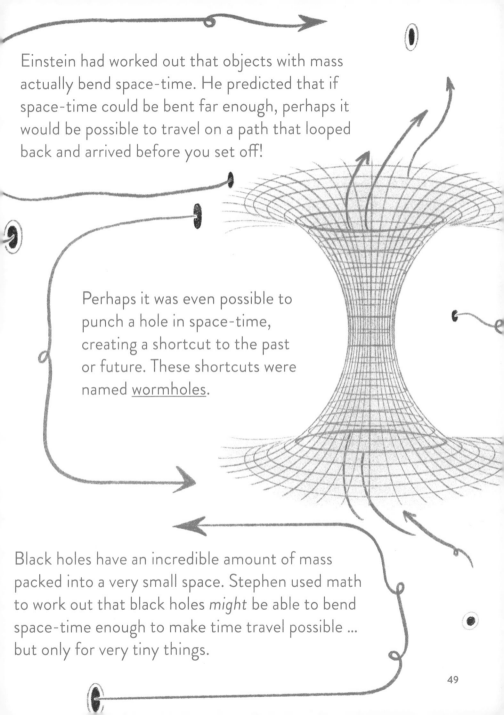

Einstein had worked out that objects with mass actually bend space-time. He predicted that if space-time could be bent far enough, perhaps it would be possible to travel on a path that looped back and arrived before you set off!

Perhaps it was even possible to punch a hole in space-time, creating a shortcut to the past or future. These shortcuts were named <u>wormholes</u>.

Black holes have an incredible amount of mass packed into a very small space. Stephen used math to work out that black holes *might* be able to bend space-time enough to make time travel possible ... but only for very tiny things.

To Stephen, human time travel seemed impossible, but he had a great sense of humor. Stephen decided to do a fun experiment, just in case! He held a party but only sent out the invitations afterward. If anyone had turned up to the party, it would have proved that time travel from the future was possible!

You are cordially invited to
a reception for time
travelers hosted by
Professor Stephen Hawking

To be held in the past, at the
University of Cambridge on
June 28, 2009

No RSVP required

Stephen had ruled out time travel, but he was very keen to try space travel. He took a trip on the "vomit comet"—a special airplane that lets people "float" like an astronaut.

The airplane does this by flying very steeply up and then down again. This makes passengers fall toward Earth at the same speed as the plane and they feel weightless for 20 or 30 seconds. Stephen grinned as he floated, and people cheered around him. He felt free.

Over time, Stephen's speech system was upgraded. He could choose words by moving his cheek. The tiny movements were picked up by a sensor on his glasses. Stephen's voice became famous around the world.

Piles of fan mail arrived for Stephen every day.
He appeared on TV and gave talks around the world.
He was even invited to open the London 2012
Paralympic Games, and an Oscar-winning movie
was made about his life.

In 2015, Stephen was excited to hear that physicists had detected gravitational waves for the first time. These may have been produced by two black holes colliding.

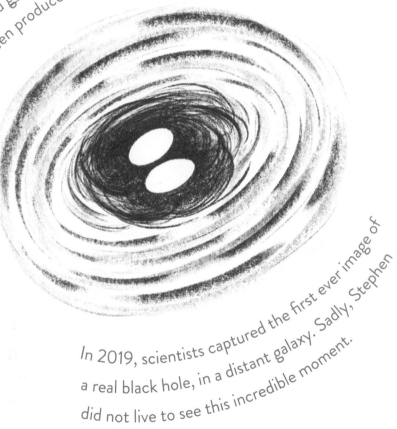

In 2019, scientists captured the first ever image of a real black hole, in a distant galaxy. Sadly, Stephen did not live to see this incredible moment.

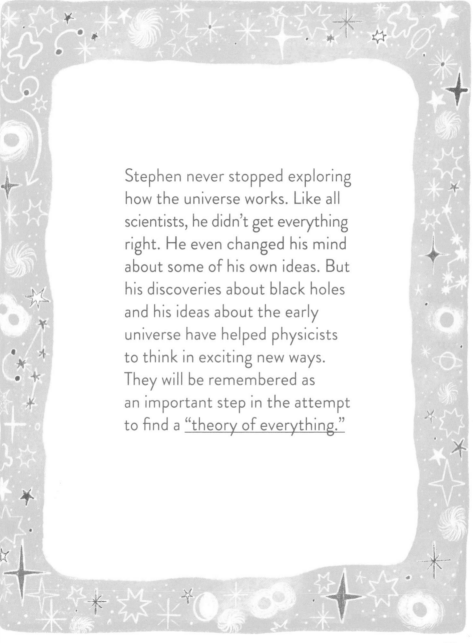

Stephen never stopped exploring how the universe works. Like all scientists, he didn't get everything right. He even changed his mind about some of his own ideas. But his discoveries about black holes and his ideas about the early universe have helped physicists to think in exciting new ways. They will be remembered as an important step in the attempt to find a <u>"theory of everything."</u>

When Stephen died on 14 March 2018, he was the world's most famous living scientist and the author of over 15 books. For more than 50 years, he had refused to let his illness and disability get in the way of the work he loved. His motto was to live life without boundaries.

Stephen is remembered for his brilliant mind and his determination. But he said that his proudest achievement was inspiring people to think more deeply about the universe, and our place in it.

TIMELINE

1942
Stephen Hawking is born on 8 January in Oxford, England, in the middle of World War Two.

1950
The Hawking family moves from London to St Albans in Hertfordshire.

1959
Stephen starts to study physics at the University of Oxford.

1974
Stephen presents his theoretical argument for the existence of Hawking radiation, shocking the scientific community. He is admitted to the Royal Society.

1974–75
Stephen moves with his family to California to take up a visiting professorship at the California Institute of Technology (Caltech).

1979
Stephen is appointed to the position of Lucasian Professor of Mathematics at the University of Cambridge.

1995
Stephen and Jane divorce, and Stephen marries his second wife, Elaine Mason.

2006
Stephen receives the Royal Society's Copley Medal, an award given for outstanding scientific research.

2007
Stephen experiences the weightlessness of space travel by taking a flight in the "vomit comet."

2014
Eddie Redmayne wins a Best Actor Oscar for his portrayal of Stephen in the movie *The Theory of Everything*.

2015
Physicists detect gravitational waves for the first time, a development that may help prove Stephen's theories.

2018
Stephen dies on 14 March, aged 76.

1962

Stephen graduates from Oxford with a first-class degree, and moves to the University of Cambridge to study cosmology.

1963

Stephen is diagnosed with amyotrophic lateral sclerosis. Doctors predict he has less than three years left to live.

1965

Stephen marries Jane Wilde on 14 July.

1984

Stephen submits the first draft of a book about the universe (later titled *A Brief History of Time*) to his publisher.

1985

On a visit to Switzerland, Stephen gets very ill and is flown home for a life-saving operation. He loses the ability to speak.

1988

A Brief History of Time: From the Big Bang to Black Holes is published and becomes a bestseller, making Stephen an international celebrity.

2009

Stephen hosts a party for time travelers— no one comes.

2012

Stephen speaks at the opening ceremony of the Paralympic Games in London.

2013

Stephen adds to his many honors and awards, receiving the Special Breakthrough Prize in Fundamental Physics.

Today

To date, *A Brief History of Time* has been translated into more than 40 languages and has sold over 25 million copies worldwide, making it one of the most successful books of all time.

GLOSSARY

atom—the smallest part of each chemical element, and the building blocks of everything else.

bestseller—a book that has sold a very large number of copies.

black hole—an area of space with incredibly strong gravity.

dense—made up of matter that is tightly packed together.

depressed—feeling sad or down or unhappy for weeks or months at a time.

eccentric—unusual or strange.

editor—a person who decides that a book should be published, and works with the author to make it as good as possible before it is published.

general theory of relativity—Albert Einstein's famous theory about time, space, and the way that objects move.

gravitational wave—a disturbance in space-time, caused, for example, by two massive objects colliding, which ripples outward as a wave.

gravity—a force between all objects made of matter, also called gravitational force. The more massive an object is (the more matter it has), the larger its gravitational force.

matter—another word for substance; unlike energy or ideas, matter is anything that takes up space and has mass.

Nobel Prizes—a set of prizes awarded each year for outstanding work in areas such as science, medicine, and literature. The prize was started by Swedish inventor Alfred Nobel in 1895.

particle accelerator—a device built to get tiny particles of matter traveling at very high speeds. Once they are traveling very quickly, the particles can be crashed into each other to learn more about them, or to produce different kinds of particles and rays that wouldn't normally be found on Earth. This makes a particle accelerator a very useful tool for finding out more about the universe.

particles—a tiny piece of matter. Atoms are particles but they are made up of even smaller particles.

phenomena—things that we can see (or hear, taste, smell, or feel) happening, and which we want to try and explain.

physicist—a scientist who studies physics.

physics—the area of science that investigates matter (what things are made of) and energy (such as heat, light, sound, and electricity). This means asking questions about every part of the universe, from tiny atoms and particles, to enormous galaxies.

pneumonia—an illness where a person's lungs become inflamed because of an infection.

research—investigating something in a careful and planned way, in order to understand it better.

singularity—an area in space where the density (how much matter is packed into that space) becomes infinite (never-ending and impossible to measure or work out). This makes singularities places where scientists cannot use the laws and theories used to explain how things behave elsewhere in the universe.

theory—a set of ideas that helps us to understand and explain some phenomenon. Theories can be tested by using them to predict how things will behave, and then carrying out observations or experiments to see if the results match the predictions. Theories are improved and sometimes replaced as we learn more about the universe and everything in it.

"theory of everything"—a single theory that could explain the nature and behavior of everything in the universe, using just one set of ideas. Physicists would like to find a theory of everything, but no one has yet.

wormhole—a passageway connecting two different parts of space-time. Wormholes have been predicted using theories such as Einstein's general theory of relativity, but no one has yet found evidence to prove that they exist. If wormholes do exist, they could act like time machines, which is an exciting idea.

INDEX

CREDITS

Photograph on page 61 courtesy of Aero Archive / Alamy Stock Photo